First World War
and Army of Occupation
War Diary
France, Belgium and Germany

74 (YEOMANRY) DIVISION
230 Infantry Brigade,
Brigade Trench Mortar Battery
1 May 1918 - 31 December 1918

WO95/3153/5

The Naval & Military Press Ltd
www.nmarchive.com
Published in association with The National Archives

Published by

The Naval & Military Press Ltd

Unit 10 Ridgewood Industrial Park,

Uckfield, East Sussex,

TN22 5QE England

Tel: +44 (0) 1825 749494

www.naval-military-press.com

www.nmarchive.com

This diary has been reprinted in facsimile from the original. Any imperfections are inevitably reproduced and the quality may fall short of modern type and cartographic standards.

© Crown Copyright
Images reproduced by permission of The National Archives, London, England, 2015.

Contents

Document type	Place/Title	Date From	Date To
Heading	WO95/3153/5 Brigade Trench Mortar Batty.		
Heading	74th Division 230th Infy Bde Trench Mortar Battery May-Dec 1918		
War Diary	Alexandria "A" Camp, Gabarry	01/05/1918	03/05/1918
War Diary	Marseilles	11/05/1918	16/05/1918
War Diary	Ponthoile	17/05/1918	22/05/1918
War Diary	Monts-En-Ternois	23/05/1918	25/05/1918
War Diary	Villers-Sir-Simon	26/05/1918	30/05/1918
War Diary	1/40000 Map 51c. Villers-Sir-Simon.	01/06/1918	30/06/1918
War Diary	Boncourt	01/07/1918	09/07/1918
War Diary	36.A.S.N	10/07/1918	10/07/1918
War Diary	P.27.b.1.3.	11/07/1918	23/07/1918
War Diary	Manqueville	24/07/1918	31/07/1918
War Diary	Sheet 36 A.S.E. 1/20.000. Ham-En-Artois.	01/08/1918	04/08/1918
War Diary	P.1.d.8.1.	05/08/1918	08/08/1918
War Diary	P.6.6.3.8.	09/08/1918	10/08/1918
War Diary	Sheet 36.A.S.E. 1/20000. P.6.b.3.8.	11/08/1918	30/08/1918
War Diary	Sheet 62.C.N.W.	31/08/1918	31/08/1918
War Diary	Reference Sheet 62C., N.E. A.29.b.5.1.	01/09/1918	01/09/1918
War Diary	B.26.d.0.5.	02/09/1918	05/09/1918
War Diary	C.29.c.2.0.	06/09/1918	11/09/1918
War Diary	D.30.c. Central	12/09/1918	18/09/1918
War Diary	F.28.c.8.3.	19/09/1918	24/09/1918
War Diary	Fouilloy	25/09/1918	30/09/1918
War Diary	Reference Sheet 36.S.W. 1/20000.	01/10/1918	01/10/1918
War Diary	X.17.a.7.5.	02/10/1918	03/10/1918
War Diary	Halpegarbe (T.7.d).	04/10/1918	05/10/1918
War Diary	Sainghin (U.H.A.5.5)	06/10/1918	10/10/1918
War Diary	U.1.d.20.75.	11/10/1918	11/10/1918
War Diary	Sheet.36.S.W.U.1D.20.75.	12/10/1918	16/10/1918
War Diary	Sheet.36.S.E.	18/10/1918	18/10/1918
War Diary	Sheet.37.	19/10/1918	19/10/1918
War Diary	N.19.a.35.08.	20/10/1918	31/10/1918
War Diary	Reference Sheet 37 1/20000. Baisieux N.19.a.35.08	01/11/1918	11/11/1918
War Diary	Sheet 38	12/11/1918	16/11/1918
War Diary	Sheet 37.	17/11/1918	30/11/1918
War Diary	Thimougies	01/12/1918	17/12/1918
War Diary	Gammerages	18/12/1918	31/12/1918

wo/95/3153/5

Braside Trenchmakers Realty.

74TH DIVISION
230TH INFY BDE

TRENCH MORTAR BATTERY
MAY - DEC 1918

Army Form C. 2118.

WAR DIARY
or
INTELLIGENCE SUMMARY.
(Erase heading not required.)

May 1918.

Place	Date	Hour	Summary of Events and Information	Remarks and references to Appendices
ALEXANDRIA Nº CAMP. SIDI BISHR	1		Medical inspection. Meat tests completed.	
	2	2 p.m.	Embarked aboard.	
	3		Steamed out of harbour with convoy.	
MARSEILLES	11	6 p.m.	Disembarked, & marched to No. 8 Rest Camp. Unloading party left at docks to entrain & guard guns & stores.	
	13	10 a.m.	Entrained, with R.F.A.	
	16⁺	1.15 a.m.	Arrived NOYELLES. Unloaded train & marched to rest camp. Reaching there about 3 a.m.	
	8ᵗʰ		Marched from rest camp to billets at PONTHOILE.	
PONTHOILE	19/21		Training each day. Manual, gun drill, aiming, gas instruction - special attention being given to the Lewis gun. Midwifes attended Gas Course at NOUVION. Being 2 days.	
	21.	10.30	Paid by Army Ord. Corps.	
	22.	1.30 a.m.	Marched to RUE STN. arriving 4 a.m., & entrained 5.30.	
		10.30	Arrived LIGNY ST. FLOCHEL, & marched to MONTS-EN-TERNOIS, arriving 1 p.m.	
MONTS-EN-TERNOIS	23/24		Training. 1 O.R. proceeded on Leave England Leave to UNITED KINGDOM.	
	25.	10.15 a.m.	Marched to VILLERS - ST. SIMON, arrived 1 p.m.	
VILLERS - ST. SIMON	26/27		Training. 1 O.R. proceeded on compassionate leave to U.K.	
	28.	8 a.m.	Physical Drill.	
		10.30	Inspection of ammunition, equipment, etc.	
		2.30 p.m.	Inspection with 154 SUPPORTS by Maj. Gen. GIRDWOOD at PERNIN.	
			1 O.R. sent on Gas Course to "J" Corps Gas School, AIRES - LES - DUSANS.	
	29/31.		Training. 1 O.R. sent to Brigade Lewis Gun School, at Bde. Hqrs.	

B. G. Whyte O. 2nd Lt.
O.C. 220th Bde. 2.0.1.B.

Army Form C. 2118.

WAR DIARY
or
INTELLIGENCE SUMMARY.
(Erase heading not required.)

230th L.T.M.B.   June 1918

Instructions regarding War Diaries and Intelligence Summaries are contained in F.S. Regs., Part II. and the Staff Manual respectively. Title pages will be prepared in manuscript.

Place	Date	Hour	Summary of Events and Information	Remarks and references to Appendices
HUGOOD 51c map 51c VILLERS-SIR-SIMON	June 1st - 2nd		Training carried out for 5½ hrs daily, except Saturday & Sunday. Physical training, Bayonet Training Manual, Gas Drill, etc. Special attention being paid to training in gas masks at all times, 1 hr long periods.	
	3rd		Capt Godbery + 7/3 (Batt) proceeded on a visit to the front line for 4 days.	
	4th			
	8th		16 men (10 from each battalion) attached to the battery for 10 days course as training for reserves to the battery.	
	9th		Gas demonstration. N.E. of cross roads at C.29.b.6.2.	
	13th		Training as above, including firing on rifle ranges. A further 16 men attached 10 days course for training as reserves.	
	14/20		Battery took part in Inter Brigade Field day.	
	18		Training as above, including firing on rifle ranges, and on Stokes Mortar Range at GIVENCHY-LES-NOBLES.	
	20		Officers + NCOs watched demonstration by SUFFOLKS + SUSSEX with tanks + Aeroplanes.	
	21		Personnel of NORFOLKS attached to battery returned to their battalion.	
	22		Training as above.	
	23		French Mortar demonstration given to Officers of the Brigade, including firing at Machine Gun emplacements + Smoke Mortar Barrage.	
	23/24		Training as above. Warning Order for move received.	
	25	6.30 am	Instructions to move at 7.15 am received.	
		7.15	Battery marched out from billeting area to LIGNY-ST FLOCHEL, arriving at 10.55 am, 1 entrained.	
		2 pm	Arrived PUCE Stn, Luentraine, + marched to BONCOURT, arriving about 6.45 pm.	
	26		Rifle + billet inspection. Board remainder of day.	
	27/30		Training as above. Lorry and street cleaning. Arrived 28th.	

B/Whitney Lieut.
for OC. 230th L.T.M.B.

Army Form C. 2118.

230th S.D.A.B.

WAR DIARY
or
INTELLIGENCE SUMMARY.
(Erase heading not required.)

July. 1918.

Instructions regarding War Diaries and Intelligence Summaries are contained in F.S. Regs., Part II. and the Staff Manual respectively. Title pages will be prepared in manuscript.

Place	Date	Hour	Summary of Events and Information	Remarks and references to Appendices
BONCOURT.	1/5th		Training: Physical drill, bayonet fighting, gun drill, etc., including practice at gun laying in Gas Masks by night.	
	6th		4 Guns took part in inter-Battalion field days consisting of battery acting as carrying party. 1 Officer proceeded on French Motor course at XIst Corps School.	
	7/8/9th		Training as above. 1 Officer proceeded on Gas course at XIst Corps school.	
	10th		Proceeded by motor lorries to HARI-EN-ARTOIS.	
36.A.S.W. P.29.6.1.3.	11th	4pm 6.30	Marched to Rear Battery Headquarters at P.29.6.1.3. (Map. 36.A. S.E. (20000)) arriving at 6 pm. "A" SECTION, under 2/Lt. Haughton went forward to gun position. Relief complete at 7.30 pm. Two forward guns at Q.13.d.99.13. & Q.13.d.9c.25. with alternative position for 1 gun at Q.14.c.35.10. 2 support guns at Q.14.a.85.25. & Q.14.a.88.30. Reserve emplacements for 2 guns at Q.19.a.40.80. & Q.19.a.45.70. Advanced Battery Headquarters at P.24.c.7.9.	
	12th		1 O.R. from gun centre.	
	13th		A few enemy aircraft about, but all driven back by A.A. fire. Heavy artillery fire from early in evening till open midnight.	
	14th		Considerable shelling of small wood in P.29.a.	
	15th		"B" section begun digging new emplacements for two forward guns.	
	16th		Work on new emplacements continued.	
	17th	3pm	"A" section relieved by "B" section.	
	18th	3.30am	Heavy 12 or 15" Yellow Cross Gas shells dropped by enemy on right of road at Q.19.a.22.34.	
		2.30pm	Intense artillery bombardment of PACAUT WOOD for 30 mins. Enemy replied with usual barrage of small calibre shells on our front & support lines. Working party from "A" section sent up to make emplacements for 4 reserve guns.	
	19th		Working party as for 18th. Party sent up to enlarge emplacements during evening. Caught by enemy shell fire. One man wounded. Capt Dougherty returned from leave.	
	20th		Working party as before.	
	21st		Very quiet all day. Guns took part in artillery barrage at midnight. Enemy raid on enemy's formation. 180 rounds fired on targets at Q.N.d.6.1. read from Q.14.a.6.1. to Q.14.a.7.8. & cross roads at Q.14.d.2.9. Enemy artillery & French mortars replied with heavy fire.	
	22nd		Working party on reserve gun emplacements. Fairly heavy enemy artillery fire in the vicinity of Q.14.a.55.20.	
MONSEUVILLE.	23rd	6pm	Relieved by 229th S.D.A.B. Battery marched to billeting area in MANGUEVILLE. 1 Officer proceeded on leave.	
	24th		Rifle inspection, kit inspection. E.A. arrived during night. Bombs dropped at distance away.	
	25th		1 hours parade, 1 hours parade later. 1 Officer & Officer proceeded on course. 1 Officer returned from course.	
	26th		Training. S.D., B.D., etc., & lecture on map reading.	
	27th		Recommissions schemes carried out by parties of N.C.O's & men. Sports being made on Canteen mess & areas.	
	28/31st		Training. 12/R. attached to Battery for 14 days course as recruits. Issued strength gas & tot new type pickel pattern 6. Eye masks.	

Army Form C. 2118.

WAR DIARY
or
INTELLIGENCE SUMMARY. 230th L.T.M.B.

August, 1918.

(Erase heading not required.)

Instructions regarding War Diaries and Intelligence Summaries are contained in F. S. Regs., Part II. and the Staff Manual respectively. Title pages will be prepared in manuscript.

Place	Date	Hour	Summary of Events and Information	Remarks and references to Appendices
SHEET 36.A.S.E. 1/20,000				
MAN.EN.ARTOIS.	1/2/3		Training. Physical drill & bayonet fighting, gun drill, & lectures.	
	4th	6.30pm	Battery relieved 231st L.T.M.B. in ST.FLORIS SECTOR. Rear positions as follows: Anti-aircraft guns at K.31.c.47.22. K.31.c.46.29. K.31.c.22.59. & K.31.c.18.90. outlet guns at P.6.b.15.50. & J.36.d.05.20. Advanced Hqrs. at P.6.b.3.8. Rear Hqrs. P.1.d.8.1. Ammunition dump P.6.a.90.60. "A" section under O.C. 2nd in line. "B" section at Rear Hqrs.	
P.1.d.8.1.	5th	3.-3.30 pm	Battery fired 40 rounds between in lines & enemy trenches in K.31.d.70.25 & 60.30. Direct hits obtained.	
	6th	5.-5.15 am	25 rounds fired on enemy trenches & machine gun post in K.31.d.70.25.	
	7th	8.30/10.30 pm	100 rounds fired into enemy trenches at K.31.d.80.12. During the action 3 tear shells & 1 barrel were rendered unserviceable.	
	8th		During the enemy's retirement, gun positions were advanced to O.3 central, Q.3.a.8.1. K.35.c.2.5. & K.35.c.8.4. Rear Hqrs. moved up to P.6.b.3.8.	
P.6.b.3.8.	9th		Two gun teams in the line relieved by two from rear Headquarters	
	10th	2.30 pm	20 rounds fired on enemy M.G. post in house at K.34a². 50.15. & enemy trenches K.34.a. 10.15.	
		2.30/3 pm	Area heavily shelled by enemy S.F. + H.E. & guns at K.35.c.7.5 ; 8. & had to be withdrawn to K.35.c.1.7. Light Aeroplanes took part in enemy reconnaissance.	
		7 pm	2 guns in line relieved by two from rear Headquarters.	

Army Form C. 2118.

WAR DIARY
or
INTELLIGENCE SUMMARY.

August 1918. 230th L.I.A.B.

(Erase heading not required.)

Place	Date	Hour	Summary of Events and Information	Remarks and references to Appendices
SHEET 36.A.S.E. 1/20000 P.6. & 3.8	11th		Very heavy bombardment along Brigade front throughout the night, during which 2 men were wounded.	
	12th	11/12 p.m.	Enemy bombardment with 5.9 H.E. Shortly after about 100 Yellow Cross Gas shells were dropped in the vicinity of Battery Keeps.	
	13th		Very quiet - nothing to report.	
	14th	1.30 a.m.	A number of Yellow Cross Gas shells fired by enemy into P.6.b. Very quiet rest of the day.	
	15th/16th		Intermittent enemy shelling - otherwise nothing to report.	
	16th	8 pm	Battery relieved by 331st L.I.A.B. & marched to billets in HAMET BILLET (P.W.6.8.2).	
	17th		Rested.	
	18th	2 km	25 O.R. under an Officer went harvesting with 16th Sussex near ROBECQ.	
	19th/26th		Harvesting each day as above.	
	26th		Relieved by 196th L.I.A.B. & marched to billets in ST. HILAIRE	
	27th		Rested	
	28th	8.30 pm	Marched to LILLERS & entrained	
	29th	pm	Arrived at NEUILLY STN. & marched to BIEZIEUX.	
	30th		Rested	
SHEET 62. C. N.W.	31st	4.30 a.m.	Proceeded by motor lorries to P. 19. c. 1. L.	

G. Stratton, Capt.

74

WAR DIARY
or
~~INTELLIGENCE SUMMARY~~
(Erase heading not required.)

Army Form C. 2118.

230th F.O.A.S.
September 1918.

Instructions regarding War Diaries and Intelligence Summaries are contained in F. S. Regs., Part II. and the Staff Manual respectively. Title pages will be prepared in manuscript.

Place	Date	Hour	Summary of Events and Information	Remarks and references to Appendices
REFERENCE SHEET 62 C, N.E. A.29.G.5.1.	1st	17.30	Battery marched up from A.29.d.5.1. to B.26.d.0.5.	
B.26.d.0.5.	2/4/5		Engaged in salvage work etc., and supplying runners for Brigade Hqrs.	
	5th 6/10		Marched to C.29.c.2.0.	
C.29.c.2.0.			Salvage work	
	11th		Marched to D.30.c. Central near TEMPLEUX DE FOSSE	
D.30.c.Central	12th 17th		Physical Drill & Regimental Fighting took morning, followed by salvage work for rest of day.	
	17th		Four guns returned to Ordnance.	
	"	18.30	"A" section under Lt. Houghton moved up to SPUR QUARRY (E.29.c.9.7.) with 10th BUFFS.	
	"		"B" section under Lt. Peel moved up to FAUSTINE QUARRY (N.S.d.) with 12th SOMERSETS.	
	18th	05.20	Both sections advanced with second wave of Infantry to first objective. By the time this was reached the wings of the attack had become restive through the mist. Sections remained here while new connection was obtained.	
			Advanced Hqrs. moved up to F.20.c. and later to F.28.c.8.3	
F.28.c.8.3	19th		"A" Section guns advanced to F.29.d.7.5. and "B" Section to F.29.b.9.4.	
	20th		Rear Hqrs. moved up from D.30.c. Central to R.S.C. Central.	
	21st		"A" Section fired 33 rounds	
	22nd	03.00	Battery relieved by 229th F.C.M.B., and eventually at Headquarters (F.28.c.8.3.)	

(2)

Army Form C. 2118.

WAR DIARY
or
INTELLIGENCE SUMMARY.

230th L.J.N.B. September 1918

(Erase heading not required.)

Instructions regarding War Diaries and Intelligence Summaries are contained in F.S. Regs., Part II. and the Staff Manual respectively. Title pages will be prepared in manuscript.

Place	Date	Hour	Summary of Events and Information	Remarks and references to Appendices
REF. SHEET 62.c.NE. F.28.c.8.3.	23rd		Enemy constantly shelled sunken road at F.28.c.8.3. with small calibre shells, wounding 3 men during the morning.	
		19.30	Brigade being relieved Battery marched to old area in D.30.c central & camped for the night.	
	24th	05.00	Rear Hqrs. rejoined remainder of Battery.	
		07.30	Marched to PERONNE Stn. and entrained for VILLERS BRETTONNEUX: on arrival marched to billets in FOUILLOY	
FOUILLOY	25th		Rested	
	26th	10.00	Marched to MERLY Stn. and entrained for LILLERS	
	27th 28/30	00.15	Arrived at LILLERS and marched to billets in ALLOUAGNE.	
			Inspection of kits, rifles, & guns.	

J Naughton 2nd Lt.

for O/ Commanding 230th L.J.N.B.

Army Form C. 2118.

October 1918.
230th L.V.M.B.

WAR DIARY
or
INTELLIGENCE SUMMARY.
(Erase heading not required.)

Instructions regarding War Diaries and Intelligence Summaries are contained in F. S. Regs., Part II. and the Staff Manual respectively. Title pages will be prepared in manuscript.

Place	Date	Hour	Summary of Events and Information	Remarks and references to Appendices
REFERENCE SHEET 36.S.W. 1/20,000.	1st	21.30	Relieved 58th C.V.M.B. in LIGNY LE PETIT SECTOR. Gun positions forward S.17.a.93.23. Rear	
X.17.a.26.	2nd		S.10.d.03.05. Battery H.Q. X.17.a.7.5. Rear H.Q. ESSARS (X.25.b.2.8.)	
			"B" SECTN. under 2/Lt. WHITFIELD moved forward to HALPEGARBE (T.7.d)	
	3rd		One gun moved on to T.7.d.10.90. 3 guns being left behind in charge of 2 men. H.qrs. moved up to	
HALPEGARBE.	4th		"B" SECTN. moved forward to SAINGHIN (U.14.a.5.5.)	
HALPEGARBE (T.7.d.)	5th		H.qrs moved up and joined "B" SECTN. at SAINGHIN. Rear H.qrs. moved to WICKES (T.12.c.4.2.)	
SAINGHIN (U.14.a.5.5.)	6th		201 shells received from D.A.C. & dumped at U.14.a.45.25. Working party of 4 Cpls. and 36 men proceeded to U.14.d.90.65. to prepare gun positions.	
	7th		Working party as above. "A" SECTN. moved up to new position with 2 guns, remainder of battery carrying up ammunition.	
	10th	14.00 to 16.00	10 Gas shells 9 C.G. dropped on GRAND RUE. SAINGHIN. Heavy shelling at intervals throughout the day. Relieved by 515th L.T.M.B. and marched to left of sector and relieved 231st L.T.M.B. "A" SECTN. took 2 guns under 2/Lt. HAUGHTON took over position at U.5.d.10.60. H.qrs. U.1.d.20.75. Rear H.qrs. T.12.c.4.7.	
U.1.d.20.75.	11th		Periodical shelling of area near H.qrs.	

(2) October 1918.

WAR DIARY
or
INTELLIGENCE SUMMARY.
(Erase heading not required.)

Army Form C. 2118.

Place	Date	Hour	Summary of Events and Information	Remarks and references to Appendices
SHEET. 36. S.W.				
U.1.d.20.75.	12th	14.00	Guns ranged on LA HAYE FARM. (O.55.d.90.75.) 6 rounds fired, retaliating to enemy mortars fire, which ceased.	
		16.30	3 rds. fired in reply to enemy mortar, which ceased fire after 2 rds.	
	13th	01.00	Guns fired 50 rds. barrage during raid by 16th SUSSEX.	
		05.30	20 rounds fired during attempted enemy raid.	
		10.00	Remaining 2 guns moved up into position with the 2 in the line.	
	14th		4 rds. fired on suspected enemy mortar.	
	15th		Gun positions as follows: U.5.c.15.64: 09.80: 00.90: 02.92. Enemy retired slightly.	
	16th		Guns withdrawn to V.1.b.9.7. in readiness to move under orders from O.C. 15th SUFFOLKS	
			Bde. Hqrs. moved back to O.32.d.40.85. Guns remained in position in P.32.c. and forward Hqrs. at V.1.b.9.7.	
SHEET. 36.S.E.	18th		Battery moved forward to Q.29.d.40.80. (SHEET 36.S.E.)	
SHEET. 37	19th		" " " " M.21.a.20.50 (SHEET. 37)	
N.19.a.35.08	20th		" " " " N.19.a.35.08 (BAISIEUX)	
	21st/23rd		Inspections, gun cleaning, & drills.	
	24th		"A" SECTN. under Lyt. HAUGHTON relieved 229th L.T.M.B. Gun positions at O.36.& 85.40. forward Hqrs.	

(3)

Army Form C. 2118.

WAR DIARY
or
INTELLIGENCE SUMMARY.
(Erase heading not required.)

Instructions regarding War Diaries and Intelligence Summaries are contained in F. S. Regs., Part II. and the Staff Manual respectively. Title pages will be prepared in manuscript.

October. 1918.

Place	Date	Hour	Summary of Events and Information	Remarks and references to Appendices
SHEET. 57.				
N.19.c.90.20.	24th		Regs. O.26.b. 20.35.: Hos. Hqrs. return N.19.c.90.20.	
	25th		27 rounds harassing fire at intervals during the night on O.27.a.65.35. and road in O.27.c.	
			During afternoon enemy put down heavy barrage on VORCQ in response to red light fired from his lines. Barrage lasted about 30 mins.	
		14.00	7 rounds ranging fired on various targets.	
		21.00	41 rounds fired on targets. M.G. at O.27.a.9.8.: cross roads O.27.a.65.35.: Enemy trenches at O.27.a.90.10.: sunken road O.29.a.4.c.	
	26th		53 rounds fired on targets as above. About 12 yellow burst shells were sent back by the enemy in reply to our fire.	
	27th		A third gun placed in position at O.26.b.85.25. to cover part of cross roads O.27.a.65.35 to 75.70. 33 rds. harassing fire on sunken road O.27.a.4.c.	
	28th		20 rds. " " " " "	
	29th		45 " " " " trenches & farm at O.27.c.6.8. 5 direct hits on.	
			Farm. Company in front reported considerably less M.G. fire since we fired.	
	30th		11 rds. on farm at O.27.c.6.8. 5 direct hits on farm, & a hay stack set on fire.	
	31st	16.00	Relieved by 231st L.T.M.B. Battery returned to BAISIEUX. Kit inspection, & short parade.	

Capel Capt
OC. 230" L.T.M.B.

230₹ L.J.A.B.
November 1918

Army Form C. 2118.

WAR DIARY
or
INTELLIGENCE SUMMARY.
(Erase heading not required.)

Instructions regarding War Diaries and Intelligence Summaries are contained in F. S. Regs., Part II. and the Staff Manual respectively. Title pages will be prepared in manuscript.

Place	Date	Hour	Summary of Events and Information	Remarks and references to Appendices
REFERENCE SHEET 39. 1/20,000				
BAISIEUX N.19.a.35.08	1		13 men from battery attached to Can Agri Staff LEMAIN. for work in TOURNAI.	
	2ⁿᵈ/8ᵗʰ		Parades (4 hours daily) & inspections	
	9ᵗʰ	15.00	Marched to billets in Moslem outskirts of TOURNAI.	
	10ᵗʰ		Short parade.	
	11ᵗʰ		Marched from TOURNAI to billets at MONTROEUL-AU-BOIS.	
SHEET 38.	12ᵗʰ		Marched to billets at LPHAMAIDE (SHEET 38)	
	13ᵗʰ/15ᵗʰ		Parades: physical exercise, & bayonet training, gun drill etc	
	16ᵗʰ		Moved to new billets at THIMOUGIES (SHEET 39).	
SHEET 32.	17ᵗʰ/30		Parades as above (3 hours daily). Lectures on Educational Scheme, etc.	

H Hamilton
Major
for O.C. 230₹ L.J.A.B.

Army Form C. 2118

WAR DIARY
or
INTELLIGENCE SUMMARY.
(Erase heading not required.)

230th L.I.A.S.
December 1918.

Place	Date	Hour	Summary of Events and Information	Remarks and references to Appendices
THIMOUGIES	1st/8th		Short parades daily, followed by sports & Recreational Evenings.	
	9th		Educational Scheme commenced. 3 hours daily. Afternoons devoted to outdoor recreation, & evening to indoor recreation.	
	10th/14th		As for 9th.	
	15th		Moved to FRASNES.	
	16th		Moved to LAISETTE (CHOY).	
	17th		Arrived at final billeting area in GAMMERAGES.	
GAMMERAGES	18th/31st		Education — Recreation as above, except on 25th & 26th.	

Alexander Lyell/Lt Col
O.C. 230th L.I.A.S.